# Patterns in the
# SNOW

by J. Clark Sawyer

Consultant: Kimberly Brenneman, PhD
National Institute for Early Education Research
Rutgers University
New Brunswick, New Jersey

**BEARPORT** PUBLISHING

New York, New York

**Credits**

Cover, © Radovan/Shutterstock; 3, © Sonja Hinrichsen/Snow Drawings–Rabbit Ears Pass/ photo Cedar Beauregard; 4–5, © Simon Bratt/Shutterstock; 6–7, © Thomas Kokta/Getty Images; 6, © Steve Byland/Shutterstock; 8–9, © WimL/Shutterstock; 10–11, © Blend Images/ Alamy; 12–13, © Shutterstock; 14–15, © David & Micha Sheldon/F1 ONLINE/SuperStock; 16–17, © Ksenia Raykova/Shutterstock; 18–19, © Sonja Hinrichsen/Snow Drawings–Rabbit Ears Pass/photo Cedar Beauregard; 20–21, © Prisma Bildagentur AG/Alamy; 22–23, © Yuliya Evstratenko/Shutterstock; 24–25, © Tom Soucek/Alaska Stock/Corbis; 26–27, © Kichigin/ Shutterstock; 28–29, © Philip Scalia/Alamy; 30A, © Image Source; 30B, © Sharon Vos–Arnold/ Getty Images; 30C, © Prisma Bildagentur AG/Alamy; 30D, © Zlikovec/Dreamstime.com; 31TL, © Design Pics Inc./Alamy; 31TR, © moizhusein/Shutterstock; 31BL, © Yuliya Evstratenko/Shutterstock; 31BR, © Topaz777/Thinkstock.

Publisher: Kenn Goin
Editor: Jessica Rudolph
Creative Director: Spencer Brinker
Design: Debrah Kaiser
Photo Researcher: Picture Perfect Professionals, LLC.

*Library of Congress Cataloging-in-Publication Data*

Clark Sawyer, J., author.
  Patterns in the snow / by J. Clark Sawyer.
    pages cm. — (Seeing patterns all around)
  Includes bibliographical references and index.
  ISBN-13: 978-1-62724-340-7 (library binding)
  ISBN-10: 1-62724-340-2 (library binding)
  1. Pattern perception—Juvenile literature. 2. Animals—Miscellanea—Juvenile literature. I. Title.
  BF294.C533 2015
  516.15—dc23
                                          2014009102

For more information, write to Bearport Publishing Company, Inc., 45 West 21st Street, Suite 3B, New York, New York 10010. Printed in the United States of America.

10 9 8 7 6 5 4 3 2 1

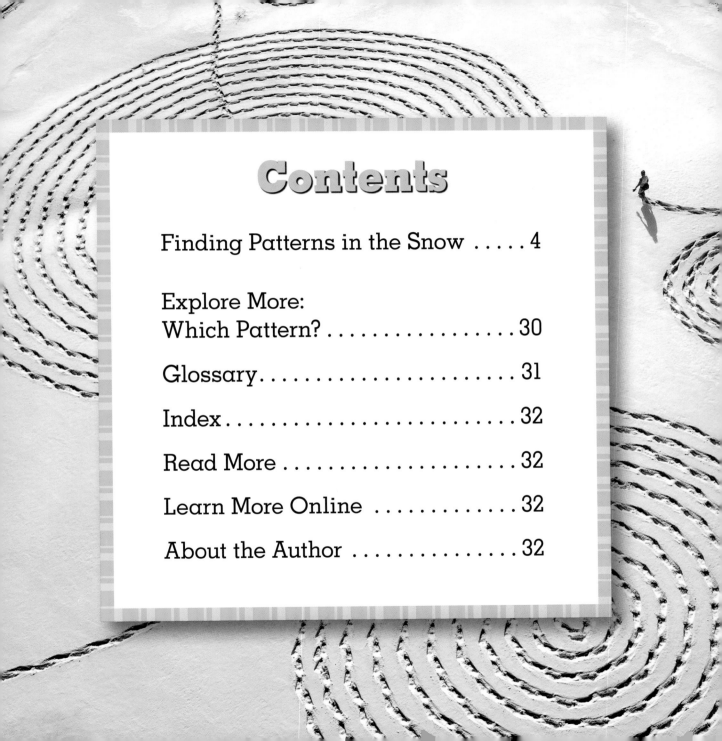

# Contents

# Finding Patterns in the Snow

Patterns can be shapes, colors, or sizes that repeat.

You can see patterns in snowy winter scenes.

A row of snowmen makes a pattern.

4

A cardinal sitting on a branch does not make a pattern.

There is just one bird.

A row of penguins,
however, makes a pattern.

Footprints make an **alternating** pattern.

Left, right.

The pattern repeats.

A family also makes an alternating pattern.

Tall, short.

This pattern repeats, too.

Mittens make a pattern.

Red, red, green, green.

The colors repeat.

The number of snowflakes on the mittens makes a pattern as well.

One, one, three, three.

An ice skater keeps warm with a striped sweater.

The colored stripes make a pattern.

Blue, gray.

A dog's scarf has colored stripes, too.

Red, white, black, white.

The pattern goes on.

Tracks in the snow swirl around.

They make a **spiral** pattern.

18

19

Skiers make wavy
patterns in the snow.

21

Black circles on a purple coat make a pattern of dots.

These are called **polka dots**.

23

A snow leopard hunts in the snow.

Its fur has black spots that are different shapes and sizes.

This is an **irregular pattern**.

Patterns can be tiny.

A snowflake has six sides.

Each side has a shape that repeats around the snowflake.

Every snowflake has a different pattern.

27

Patterns can also be huge.

What repeated shape do you see in this ice castle?

In winter, look around to find patterns in the snow!

29

# Explore More:
## Which Pattern?

Look at the pictures. Each one shows a kind of pattern that can be found in a winter scene. Match each pattern with the correct picture.

1. polka-dot pattern

3. striped pattern

2. wave pattern

4. irregular pattern

Answers are on page 32.

# Glossary

**alternating** (AWL-tur-*nayt*-ing) changing back and forth, such as between two colors

**irregular pattern** (ih-REG-yuh-lur PAT-urn) a pattern that has one or more similar parts unequal in size, shape, or in the way they are arranged

**polka dots** (POH-kuh DOTS) a pattern that has dots of the same size that are evenly spaced

**spiral** (SPYE-ruhl) winding or circling around a center

# Index

# Read More

**Harris, Trudy.** *Pattern Bugs.* Brookfield, CT: Millbrook (2001).

**Olson, Nathan.** *Animal Patterns.* Mankato, MN: Capstone (2007).

# Learn More Online

To learn more about patterns in the snow, visit
**www.bearportpublishing.com/SeeingPatternsAllAround**

# About the Author

J. Clark Sawyer lives in Connecticut. She has edited and written many books about history, science, and nature for children.

# Answers for Page 30:

1. B; 2. C; 3. A; 4. D